The Power of Inspiration

*Every day I make a choice to transcend the
negative and use every moment there is breath in
this body to positively impact the world around me.*

~ PREETHI SRINIVASAN ~

RANDI TOMCHIN

iUniverse®

The Power of Inspiration

iUniverse books may be ordered through booksellers or by contacting:

iUniverse
1663 Liberty Drive
Bloomington, IN 47403
www.iuniverse.com
844-349-9409

Because of the dynamic nature of the Internet, any web addresses or links contained in this book may have changed since publication and may no longer be valid. The views expressed in this work are solely those of the author and do not necessarily reflect the views of the publisher, and the publisher hereby disclaims any responsibility for them.

Any people depicted in stock imagery provided by Getty Images are models, and such images are being used for illustrative purposes only.
Certain stock imagery © Getty Images.

ISBN: 978-1-6632-3584-8 (sc)
ISBN: 978-1-6632-3646-3 (e)

Library of Congress Control Number: 2022903609

Print information available on the last page.

iUniverse rev. date: 03/07/2022

Introduction

In 2009, I started a consulting practice called Enrichment Inc. with this declared mission: *Opening Minds. Awakening Hearts.* It was the fulfillment of a deep desire that had stirred me for many years: to use my talents and experiences to be of service and guide others on a path to Awakening.

As I was beginning to build my social media presence, I frequently posted positive, inspiring quotations I found along the way. There weren't a lot of people doing that at the time, and a number of readers started calling me "The Quote Girl."

People responded favorably to the encouraging statements I shared, often telling me that one or another was just what they needed to read that day. I began to realize that, in small ways, we can inspire others, and we may help someone smile – even if just for a moment. After all, our lives are made up only of moments, so the more uplifting ones we experience, the better!

Recently, as I was writing my book *An Awakening Heart,* someone suggested I pull together some of my favorite quotations and compile them in a little volume that a person could carry with them and open when they needed a moment of joy or a chance to reflect. That was the seed of *The Power of Inspiration.*

Of course, words and quotations – even the finest and most astute – are not all-encompassing Truth in and of themselves; they can, however, point us in the right direction as we seek truth for ourselves. When I've had dark periods in my life, or even just rough spots in a day, reminding myself with sayings like these has helped me realign and reconnect with the Light, with all that is pure and true. That's why I'm sharing these quotes – some amusing, others joyful, or wise – so they may do the same for you.

My hope for both of my books is to inspire and encourage all who read them, to "open minds and awaken hearts."

How to Use This Book

This book is meant to be carried with you as you go about your day. If you face a challenging moment, or find yourself with a few spare minutes to get in touch with your inner self, open it at random, allowing your intuition to guide you. Often the first quote you turn to offers just what you seek . . . or you might need to scan several pages to find words that address what's on your mind. You can also go back to a quotation you've read before and delve deeper into it. If you read a quotation that lifts your mood, brings new insight, or deepens your understanding of something you may already know, you might jot down a few thoughts of reflection. You might even like to date your notes so you can look back later and see where your journey of growth has taken you. The key is to trust that you will always be guided to what will serve you best.

You will notice that some quotations use gender-specific terms like "a man" or "he." While the statement may have been written or said that way (most likely in an earlier time), my intention for these selections is to be meaningful and inspirational to everyone, of any and all identities, now or in the future. Simply substitute the nouns or pronouns that you most relate to and are most comfortable with.

Finally, you may have seen or heard one or another of these quotations credited to an author other than the one I've indicated. I've done my best to identify the originator of each statement, although others may have used, presented, or published the same (or very similar) thought or statement. On some occasions I've used an updated version of an older quotation and attributed it to the author of the newer version.

Sometimes quotations are widely misattributed, particularly on the internet, where those passing them along may not always have researched the authorship. And sometimes it's not possible to pin down authoritative evidence of original authorship, even with careful searching. Given these challenges, I've attributed each statement as authentically as I reasonably can. In cases where I could not find credible evidence of authorship, I've used the designation "Author Unknown."

With all that said, follow your intuition. Most of all, use this book as an aid in your quest for continuing personal growth, self-knowledge, and fulfillment.

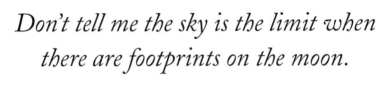

Don't tell me the sky is the limit when there are footprints on the moon.

~ PAUL BRANDT ~

THOUGHTS OF
Reflection

Be a rainbow in someone's cloud.

~ MAYA ANGELOU ~

THOUGHTS OF
Reflection

_____

_____

_____

_____

_____

_____

_____

_____

_____

_____

_____

_____

_____

_____

_____

_____

_____

Dip into your own soul. Find your own truth. What calls to your heart? What moves your spirit? Make your life dance to the song of your own essence.

~ DIANA HAYMOND ~

THOUGHTS OF
Reflection

_____

_____

_____

_____

_____

_____

_____

_____

_____

_____

_____

_____

_____

_____

_____

_____

_____

The fires of suffering become the light of consciousness.

~ ECKHART TOLLE ~

THOUGHTS OF
Reflection

The moon taught me: It's okay to go through phases.
The Sun taught me: No matter how many times you go down, keep rising.

~ AUTHOR UNKNOWN ~

THOUGHTS OF
Reflection

_____

_____

_____

_____

_____

_____

_____

_____

_____

_____

_____

_____

_____

_____

_____

_____

_____

_____

_____

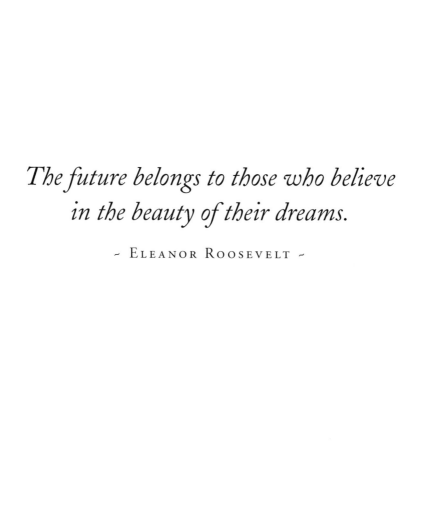

*The future belongs to those who believe
in the beauty of their dreams.*

~ ELEANOR ROOSEVELT ~

THOUGHTS OF
Reflection

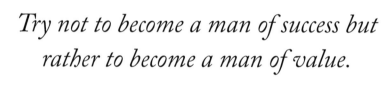

Try not to become a man of success but rather to become a man of value.

~ ALBERT EINSTEIN ~

THOUGHTS OF
Reflection

How cool is it that the same Higher Power who created mountains, oceans and galaxies looked at you and thought the world needed one of you, too.

~ Author Unknown ~

THOUGHTS OF
Reflection

_____

_____

_____

_____

_____

_____

_____

_____

_____

_____

_____

_____

_____

_____

_____

_____

_____

I will look to the past with appreciation for the lessons I was provided, and look to the future with the intent of understanding how those lessons have helped enlighten me.

~ SHIRLEY MACLAINE ~

THOUGHTS OF
Reflection

_____

_____

_____

_____

_____

_____

_____

_____

_____

_____

_____

_____

_____

_____

_____

_____

_____

_____

_____

*Laughter is a tranquilizer without
side effects. Please take daily.*

~ ARNOLD H GLASGOW ~

THOUGHTS OF
Reflection

_____

_____

_____

_____

_____

_____

_____

_____

_____

_____

_____

_____

_____

_____

_____

_____

_____

_____

*You are braver than you believe,
stronger than you seem, and smarter
than you think.*

~ A. A. Milne ~

THOUGHTS OF
Reflection

_____

_____

_____

_____

_____

_____

_____

_____

_____

_____

_____

_____

_____

_____

_____

_____

_____

_____

*Even after all this time, the Sun has
never said to the Earth: "You owe me."
Look what happens with love like
that. It lights the whole sky.*

~ HAFEZ ~

THOUGHTS OF
Reflection

Authenticity is the daily practice of letting go of who we think we're supposed to be and embracing who we are.

~ BRENÉ BROWN ~

THOUGHTS OF
Reflection

If you're still looking for that one person who can change your life, take a look in the mirror.

~ ROMAN PRICE ~

THOUGHTS OF
Reflection

_____

_____

_____

_____

_____

_____

_____

_____

_____

_____

_____

_____

_____

_____

_____

_____

_____

_____

_____

Clouds come floating into my life, no longer to carry rain or usher storm, but to add color to my sunset sky.

~ RABINDRANATH TAGORE ~

THOUGHTS OF
Reflection

_____

_____

_____

_____

_____

_____

_____

_____

_____

_____

_____

_____

_____

_____

_____

_____

_____

_____

Just when the caterpillar thought her life was over, she became a butterfly.

~ AUTHOR UNKNOWN ~

THOUGHTS OF
Reflection

_____

_____

_____

_____

_____

_____

_____

_____

_____

_____

_____

_____

_____

_____

_____

_____

_____

*Don't judge each day by the harvest
you reap but by the seeds that you
plant.*

~ ROBERT LOUIS STEVENSON ~

THOUGHTS OF
Reflection

Be yourself; everyone else is already taken.

~ OSCAR WILDE ~

THOUGHTS OF
Reflection

Life is not a problem to be solved, but
a reality to be experienced.

~ SOREN KIERKEGAARD ~

THOUGHTS OF
Reflection

_____

_____

_____

_____

_____

_____

_____

_____

_____

_____

_____

_____

_____

_____

_____

_____

Trust the wait. Embrace the uncertainty. Enjoy the beauty of becoming. When nothing is certain, anything is possible.

~ MANDY HALE ~

THOUGHTS OF
Reflection

_____

_____

_____

_____

_____

_____

_____

_____

_____

_____

_____

_____

_____

_____

_____

_____

_____

_____

*Have the courage to follow your heart
and intuition. They somehow already
know what you truly want to become.*

~ STEVE JOBS ~

THOUGHTS OF

Reflection

Life's beautiful paradox: once you learn to let go, you gain everything you were holding on to.

~ AUTHOR UNKNOWN ~

THOUGHTS OF
Reflection

One drop of joy has the power to transform oceans of anger, fear and jealousy.

~ KEVIN RYERSON ~

THOUGHTS OF
Reflection

You are here to make a contribution that flows uniquely through you. When you discover that gift, and make it central to your life, you become naturally brilliant and everything else falls into place.

~ Arjuna Ardagh ~

THOUGHTS OF
Reflection

_____

_____

_____

_____

_____

_____

_____

_____

_____

_____

_____

_____

_____

_____

_____

_____

Kindness is the language which the deaf can hear and the blind can see.

~ MARK TWAIN ~

THOUGHTS OF
Reflection

Due to personal reasons, I will be shining brightly and unapologetically for the foreseeable future.

~ AUTHOR UNKNOWN ~

THOUGHTS OF
Reflection

_____

_____

_____

_____

_____

_____

_____

_____

_____

_____

_____

_____

_____

_____

_____

_____

_____

_____

We delight in the beauty of the butterfly, but rarely admit the changes it has gone through to achieve that beauty.

~ MAYA ANGELOU ~

THOUGHTS OF
Reflection

If we did all the things we are capable of, we would literally astound ourselves.

~ THOMAS A. EDISON ~

THOUGHTS OF
Reflection

I will not rescue you, for you are not powerless. I will not fix you, for you are not broken. I will not heal you, for I see you in your wholeness. I will walk with you through the darkness, as you remember your light.

~ AUTHOR UNKNOWN ~

THOUGHTS OF
Reflection

What lies behind us, and what lies before us, are tiny matters compared to what lies within us.

~ Henry Stanley Haskins ~

THOUGHTS OF
Reflection

_____

_____

_____

_____

_____

_____

_____

_____

_____

_____

_____

_____

_____

_____

_____

_____

_____

Every experience, no matter how bad it seems, holds within it a blessing of some kind. The goal is to find it.

~ AUTHOR UNKNOWN ~

THOUGHTS OF
Reflection

_____

_____

_____

_____

_____

_____

_____

_____

_____

_____

_____

_____

_____

_____

_____

_____

_____

_____

_____

When you come to the end of your rope,
tie a knot and hang on.

~ THOMAS JEFFERSON ~

THOUGHTS OF

Reflection

_____

_____

_____

_____

_____

_____

_____

_____

_____

_____

_____

_____

_____

_____

_____

_____

*Enlightenment is when a wave
realizes it is the ocean.*

~ THICH NHAT HANH ~

THOUGHTS OF
Reflection

Be gentle when she shows you her scars. It takes more courage to remove one's armor, than to assemble it.

~ STŘELOU ~

THOUGHTS OF
Reflection

We are all threads in a magnificent tapestry, each one necessary to make the whole vibrant and complete.

~ RANDI TOMCHIN ~

THOUGHTS OF
Reflection

*The mind will not always remember
exactly what happened, but the heart
will always remember the feeling.*

~ Author Unknown ~

THOUGHTS OF
Reflection

_____

_____

_____

_____

_____

_____

_____

_____

_____

_____

_____

_____

_____

_____

_____

_____

_____

*May your walls know joy, every room
hold laughter, and every window open
to great possibility.*

~ MARY ANNE RADMACHER ~

THOUGHTS OF
Reflection

We do not need magic to transform our world. We carry all of the power we need inside ourselves already.

~ J.K. ROWLING ~

THOUGHTS OF
Reflection

The best and most beautiful things in the world cannot be seen or even touched. They must be felt with the heart.

~ HELEN KELLER ~

THOUGHTS OF
Reflection

To be fully alive, fully human, and completely awake is to be continually thrown out of the nest.

~ PEMA CHODRON ~

THOUGHTS OF
Reflection

_____

_____

_____

_____

_____

_____

_____

_____

_____

_____

_____

_____

_____

_____

_____

_____

_____

_____

In a society that has you counting money, pounds, calories and steps, be a rebel and count your blessings instead.

~ LISA HECKMAN ~

THOUGHTS OF
Reflection

Do just once what others say you can't do, and you will never pay attention to their limitations again.

~ JAMES R. COOK ~

THOUGHTS OF
Reflection

Don't give up on the person you're becoming.

~ AUTHOR UNKNOWN ~

THOUGHTS OF
Reflection

One day, in retrospect, the years of struggle will strike you as the most beautiful.

~ SIGMUND FREUD ~

THOUGHTS OF
Reflection

I do not at all understand the mystery of grace--only that it meets us where we are but does not leave us where it found us.

~ ANNE LAMOTT ~

THOUGHTS OF
Reflection

_____

_____

_____

_____

_____

_____

_____

_____

_____

_____

_____

_____

_____

_____

_____

_____

In a gentle way, you can shake the world.

~ MAHATMA GANDHI ~

THOUGHTS OF
Reflection

_____

_____

_____

_____

_____

_____

_____

_____

_____

_____

_____

_____

_____

_____

_____

_____

_____

The privilege of a lifetime is being who you are.

~ CARL JUNG ~

THOUGHTS OF
Reflection

_____

_____

_____

_____

_____

_____

_____

_____

_____

_____

_____

_____

_____

_____

_____

_____

_____

Never go in search of love. Go in search of life. And life will find you the love you seek.

~ ATTICUS ~

THOUGHTS OF
Reflection

Ocean air, salty hair, not a care: take me there.

~ AUTHOR UNKNOWN ~

THOUGHTS OF
Reflection

_____

_____

_____

_____

_____

_____

_____

_____

_____

_____

_____

_____

_____

_____

_____

_____

Happiness is free. Help yourself.

~ NHAT HANH ~

THOUGHTS OF
Reflection

_____

_____

_____

_____

_____

_____

_____

_____

_____

_____

_____

_____

_____

_____

_____

_____

_____

Blessed is he who has learned to admire but not envy, to follow but not imitate, to praise but not flatter, and to lead but not manipulate.

~ WILLIAM ARTHUR WARD ~

THOUGHTS OF
Reflection

_____

_____

_____

_____

_____

_____

_____

_____

_____

_____

_____

_____

_____

_____

_____

_____

_____

Others can stop you temporarily.
You are the only one who can do it
permanently.

~ ZIG ZIGLAR ~

THOUGHTS OF
Reflection

*Forget the pain the experience brought,
but never forget the lesson gained.*

~ RANDI TOMCHIN ~

THOUGHTS OF
Reflection

It's time to start living the life you've imagined.

~ HENRY JAMES ~

THOUGHTS OF
Reflection

In any given moment, we have two options: to step forward into growth, or step back into safety.

~ ABRAHAM MASLOW ~

THOUGHTS OF
Reflection

_____

_____

_____

_____

_____

_____

_____

_____

_____

_____

_____

_____

_____

_____

_____

_____

_____

A lot of things broke my heart, but they fixed my vision.

~ Author Unknown ~

THOUGHTS OF
Reflection

Those who flow as life flows know they need no other force.

~ LAO TZU ~

THOUGHTS OF
Reflection

_____

_____

_____

_____

_____

_____

_____

_____

_____

_____

_____

_____

_____

_____

_____

_____

_____

There will always be someone who can't see your worth. Don't let that be you!

~ MEL ROBBINS ~

THOUGHTS OF
Reflection

Be realistic. Plan for a miracle.

~ BHAGWAN SHREE RAJNEESH ~

THOUGHTS OF
Reflection

_____

_____

_____

_____

_____

_____

_____

_____

_____

_____

_____

_____

_____

_____

_____

_____

_____

Remember there's no such thing as a small act of kindness. Every act creates a ripple with no logical end.

~ Scott Adams ~

THOUGHTS OF
Reflection

_____

_____

_____

_____

_____

_____

_____

_____

_____

_____

_____

_____

_____

_____

_____

_____

_____

About the Author

Randi Tomchin is a writer, spiritual entrepreneur, transformation facilitator based in New York City. She is the founder and president of ENRICHMENT, INC., a consulting practice she created in 2009 to offer transformational experiences to those who desire a new reality and a more fulfilling approach to life.

Randi has studied and worked with many influential transformation leaders of our time, including Gregg Braden, Kevin Ryerson, and John Harvey Gray. These remarkable teachers profoundly enriched her life and continue to fuel her passion to share their wisdom – and the wisdom of others like them – with all who wish to embark on a journey to Awakening and remembering their truest selves.

Previously, Randi enjoyed a successful career in the corporate world, applying her strong customer focus, keen sales ability, and attention to detail to developing, managing, and promoting high-level executive events attended by leading media figures and renowned corporate officers. Later, in the field of training and recruitment, she combined those abilities with her talent for business development, and her knack for building and maintaining excellent client relationships, to help others achieve their life and career goals.

Currently, Randi is working on *An Awakening Heart,* a book about her own spiritual journey, also due out in 2022. To learn more about Randi and her work, visit Enrichmentinc.com.

Printed in the United States
by Baker & Taylor Publisher Services